# BIBLE STUDY PERSPECTIVES

# Bible Study Perspectives

## Volume I: Genesis

**Shanelle E. Dupree, JD**

Scripture quotations are taken from the Holy Bible, New Living Translation, copyright ©1996, 2004, 2015 by Tyndale House Foundation. Used by permission of Tyndale House Publishers, a Division of Tyndale House Ministries, Carol Stream, Illinois 60188. All rights reserved.

ISBN: 978-1-7352487-0-7

# ACKNOWLEDGMENTS

To my law school sweetheart, Mark Dupree-

Darling, I will always honor the God in you that ALWAYS shows up on the outside of you. The connection we have is out of this world, and I'm so grateful we are doing life together. I simply adore and appreciate you.

To our children Layla, Mark II, Lilly, and Micah-

We are building a legacy of purpose for not only you, but for generations to come. Mama and Daddy are excited to cultivate and support the greatness God has within each of you.

# What is *Bible Study Perspectives*?

*Bible Study Perspectives* (BSP) is a Christian Bible study guide examining God's word through the complicated lens of the law, family, media, and cultural conversations. *BSP* will increase the readership and curiosity of God's word by retelling key biblical principles and connecting it with issues we all face.

All the possible family drama, abuse, and jealousy ever imagined is documented and written in the Bible. Yet God continues to use flawed people and situations to yield beautiful concepts such as love, connection, loyalty, restoration, purpose, and forgiveness.

Have you struggled to connect to God's word in a meaningful and long-lasting way? Do you find your Bible study times are spent aimlessly searching through the scriptures with no true end goal? Bible Study Perspectives uses the Perspectives Study Method to dive deep into God's word.

*BSP* is not for those who believe every person in the Bible was perfect. *BSP* is not for those who dislike questions. *BSP* will not provide all the answers but will serve as a catalyst to discussion and active application to God's word. *BSP* will also highlight cultural conversations. The church must begin having a dialogue regarding race and disparities within our communities.

I would encourage *BSP* participants to say this simple prayer before they begin each lesson/perspective: "Lord, bless this Bible study; allow my heart to remain open, your word to change my life, and for me to see you in everything. In Jesus's name. Amen."

## What is the Perspectives Study Method?
The Perspectives Study Method is a system used to connect principles of God's word in your heart and mind by relating the lessons to people, places, events, or things. If you have struggled to consistently study the word of God, this method is for you. Plan on falling in love with God's word and seeing God's word in everything.

**Step 1: Break it down.** Each lesson is small yet power-packed with principles and lessons to apply to your life.

**Step 2: Consistency.** Examine your life and understand where you can commit to spending at least fifteen minutes a day for five days consuming God's word... and then do it.

**Step 3: Analyze. Apply.** God's word is analyzed and applied by using these steps: Connecting God's word to something you like/enjoy. Connecting God's word to something you love. Connecting God's word to something you respect. Connecting God's word to something important to you.

## How to Read the Perspectives

Each lesson is called a perspective. The perspectives are divided into ten lessons, which may be taught or read in as little as ten weeks or spread over forty weeks. Feel free to consume each perspective on the schedule that works best for you, your family, small group, church, or organization. Remember this is not a race. Take your time and dive deep. *Bible Study Perspectives* will delve into the word of God by focusing on the book of Genesis in volume I. We are discussing biblical principles through the complicated lens of the family, legal, media, and cultural perspectives.

### Format for *Bible Study Perspectives*
- The title of the Perspective (lesson) and the connected scriptures
- The name of a relevant movie or book
- God's word retold
- Questions for discussion
- Present-day perspective
- "BSP Takeaway"
- Cultural conversation starters
- Legal case
- Additional relevant scriptures for review
- Capture your perspective and share if time allows

# Table of Contents

# Foreword

I recall when Mark and I graduated law school. It happened at the beginning of the Great Recession, and there were no legal jobs available. We were recently married, deeply in love, and in a tremendous amount of law school debt. After applying for dozens of positions, I was eventually hired at a major law firm as a redactor. I was grateful for the job; however, I had just spent six and a half years earning an undergraduate degree in political science, a Juris Doctor degree, and passed the Kansas bar exam, and the only job I was able to secure was pouring through thousands of legal documents and hiding words that revealed personal information. It was a mind-numbing work, and my mind often wandered. Through this experience I grew closer to God. I could listen to CDs at my desk. I decided to use this time to build my faith. This meant I needed to read and hear the word of God. As a result, I purchased *The Bible Experience*. It is an audio Bible read in drama form by actors and singers with professional sound effects. It is wonderfully produced. I began to really understand the history of God's word. It also made the Bible come alive. I began to view the writings not as ancient teachings that were not applicable to my life but rather as living and breathing teachings with relevance. Fast-forward thirteen years later, I am laced with years of experience working as a lawyer in the foster care system and high-conflict custody cases; seasoned as an instructor, a wife, and mother of four; a current Bible study teacher; and administrator in a social service agency. I am meshing my perspectives to discuss the word of God through this work entitled *Bible Study Perspectives*. God's word is truly the light of this world and in it we find guidance and purpose. May you see God's word in everything.

# Perspective 1—A Path for Restoration: Genesis 3:20–24

*The Pursuit of Happyness* a 2006 movie

The first eviction can be traced back to Adam and Eve. They were evicted by the ultimate judge: God. Angels guarded the entrance to the Garden of Eden, so there was no way Adam and Eve were sneaking back in. Their eviction was a result of their own disobedience; they ate from the only tree from which Adam was told not to eat.[1] Yet Adam and Eve were still vital in populating the earth, which allowed humanity an opportunity to restore its relationship with God. What if Adam and Eve had given up? What if they would have stopped "being fruitful and multiplying"?

- Have you ever disappointed someone you care about?
- Should family members always have a path for restoration?
- How do you recover and restore trust?

**A pastor's daughter's perspective:** My parents were very particular with the company my brothers and I kept and the places we went. I began to feel as though my "good works" were not appreciated, and I was missing out. This was absolutely the devil speaking to me, and I was fifteen and listening attentively. I began sneaking out of the house and eventually was caught. Life changed overnight. My door was removed from the hinges, trust was lost, my parents were upset, my brothers were disappointed, and I felt completely alone. I remember one day my mom came into my room (no knocking necessary, as there was no door), and she looked at me and said, "You know we love you." As simple as that statement was—I had forgotten. Because of the mess that I had caused, I had forgotten that despite my bad decisions, I was still loved. I began seeking

---

1  See Genesis 3:1–19

how I could earn their trust back. Ultimately, I graduated high school early, attended college classes my last year in high school, maintained a 4.0 grade point average, and worked two jobs over the summers, earning my family's trust *and* my door back. Mistakes don't mean we don't still have a purpose.

**BSP takeaway:** Everyone makes mistakes. Are we creating pathways for restoration within our families?

**Legal case:** Sometimes people are forced to pay for others' mistakes. Four families were evicted from the Oakland Housing Authority because a household member, guest, or person under the tenant's "control" engaged in drug-related criminal activity. For example, one of the tenants appealing the eviction was a grandmother whose grandsons were found smoking marijuana on the property. Ultimately, the Supreme Court ruled they could be evicted—even if they had no idea the drug-related activities were occurring. *Department of Housing and Urban Development v. Rucker, 535 U.S. 125 (2002)*

**Cultural conversation:** Many Americans lost their homes and livelihoods during the Great Depression. President Roosevelt implemented the New Deal to generate economic stability. As a result, the National Housing Act of 1934 was passed by Congress. A federally guaranteed and low-cost home loan program was established and provided a path to homeownership and a way to build wealth. The agency responsible for administering the program and deciding who to grant a home loan divided cities into green (good businessmen and good area), blue (still desirable, and expected to remain stable areas), yellow (definitely declining and usually close to red areas), and red (undesirable locations where foreign born, blacks, and poor whites lived) zones.[2] Families who lived in the green and blue zones were granted loans and able to purchase single-family homes in the suburbs. This was not true for yellow and red zones. This "redlining" caused businesses, such as banks and grocery stores, to migrate toward the blue and green neighborhoods. Ninety-eight percent of the housing loans were given to white families while the program was active. The results of this were disastrous for people of color and poor whites. Not only were those in the "red zones" unable to secure a home loan, the Federal Housing Authority (FHA) lenders were subsidizing developers to build in white areas with the

2   https://www.smithsonianmag.com/history/
how-federal-government-intentionally-racially-segregated-american-cities-180963494/

rule they were not to sell to people of color. The effects are generationally, economically, educationally, and environmentally traumatizing for these communities.[3] There was minimal investment in schools because of low property taxes, and the red zones were typically located near hazardous environmental sites. This resulted in nearly thirty years of building and investing in white neighborhoods, while areas that were redlined had limited resources and limited opportunities.

**Scriptures for further reading and reflection:**
- "This means that anyone who belongs to Christ has become a new person. The old life is gone; a new life has begun!" **2 Corinthians 5:17**
- "Dear brothers and sisters, if another believer is overcome by some sin, you who are godly should gently and humbly help that person back onto the right path. And be careful not to fall into the same temptation yourself. Share each other's burdens, and in this way obey the law of Christ. If you think you are too important to help someone, you are only fooling yourself. You are not that important." **Galatians 6:1–3**
- "Instead, be kind to each other, tenderhearted, forgiving one another, just as God through Christ has forgiven you." **Ephesians 4:32**

**What's your perspective?**

---

3   Fullilove, Mindy. "Redlining Trauma." *Race, Poverty & the Environment*, vol. 21, no. 2, 2017, pp. 84–86. JSTOR, www.jstor.org/stable/44687766. Accessed 22 Nov. 2020.

# Perspective 2—Murder among Siblings: Genesis 4:1–16

*The Lion King* a 1994 & 2019 movie

Directly after Adam and Eve were evicted from the Garden of Eden, we meet their sons Cain and Abel. In Genesis 4 they are offering gifts to God. Cain gave a "C-" gift to God. His younger brother, Abel, gave an "A+" gift to God. God rejected Cain's gift but accepted Abel's gift. This angered Cain, and he stayed angry. Cain murdered his brother Abel and was evicted (like his parents in Genesis 3) and cursed to wander the earth.

- Have you lost a family member to violence?
- What effect did it have on you or someone you may know?
- Does it matter how a person dies, or just that they died?

**Legal perspective:** A child was murdered by the mother's boyfriend. I was appointed to represent the biological father in the child-in-need-of-care case. The mother and father were divorced and had five children together. The mother's boyfriend was charged with killing one of the children. The mother believed the boyfriend was innocent. The children were removed from the mother's home because of something called "failure to protect." The mother was visiting the boyfriend in jail and trying to get the other children to change their witness statements (they witnessed the murder). While in child-in-need-of-care court, the father and I worked with the social service agency, and ultimately my client's four children were placed with him. The trauma and guilt the father and children experienced was gut-wrenching to witness. Ultimately the children and father received the help they needed and were able to move forward as a family, never forgetting their slain loved one. It made a difference for everyone in the case that the child was murdered. Only God can heal certain wounds.

**BSP takeaway:** Violence can destroy an entire family. If you or someone you know has anger issues, consider receiving help.

**Cultural conversation:** The myth of "black-on-black" crime is deeply rooted in a misunderstanding of the actual issue.[4] The truth is, people who live around one another typically kill one another. Additionally, spreading the myth that black people are inherently more violent than the rest of the population is a racist idea that has been used to justify slavery, colonization, Jim Crow laws, and ultimately the unequal treatment of blacks. What is linked within the discussion of violence is poverty. Poor whites and blacks commit crime at the same rate. There is no "violent" gene.[5] This is an important conversation to have within our churches, homes, and communities because it matters how we think and treat one another.

**Scriptures for further reading and reflection:**
- "An angry person starts fights; a hot-tempered person commits all kinds of sin." **Proverbs 29:22**
- "Control your temper, for anger labels you a fool." **Ecclesiastes 7:9**
- "A gentle answer deflects anger, but harsh words make tempers flare." **Proverbs 15:1**

**What's your perspective?**

---

4  Headley, Bernard D. "'Black on Black' Crime: The Myth and the Reality." *Crime and Social Justice*, no. 20, 1983, pp. 50–62. *JSTOR*, www.jstor.org/stable/29766208. Accessed 21 Nov. 2020.

5  Braga, Anthony A., and Brunson, Rod K. The Police and Public Discourse on "Black-on-Black" Violence. New Perspectives in Policing Bulletin. Washington, D.C.: U.S. Department of Justice, National Institute of Justice, 2015. NCJ 248588

# Perspective 3—Losing a Black-Haired: Genesis 4:1–16

*Losing Isaiah* a 1996 movie

Adam and Eve lost both of their sons. Cain was cursed to wander the earth, and Abel was murdered by his brother. Any death of a child is a traumatic experience for the entire family.

- Does our culture do a good job with supporting parents who have lost children?
- What do you think would help parents who experience this type of loss?
- Does your response change if the child dies of a drug overdose, in prison, or by suicide?

**Cultural perspective:** There is no term in the United States for a parent who has lost a child. The Chinese culture has a term that means "the gray-haired should not bury the black-haired." Karla Holloway, a Duke professor, wrote an article in 2009 to reflect on the lack of identifying language for parents who have lost a child. She found a word while searching the Sanskrit language. Professor Holloway found *vilomah*, which means, "against the natural order," as in, "Our children should not precede us in death."[6]

**BSP takeaway:** If you have lost a child, God sees your pain and hears you. He is always working to bind up your wounds.

**A legal case:** There are many ways to lose a child. In a Missouri case, a mother's parental rights were terminated because she medically abused her child by subjecting him to numerous unnecessary medications and testing and allowing her ex-boyfriend to sexually

---

6  Holloway, Karla. "Giving a Name to the Pain of Losing a Child." https://www.npr.org/templates/story/story.php?storyId=5511147. Accessed 14 May 2020.

and physically abuse her child. She did not provide child support. She was incarcerated on charges of first-degree murder.

*In re S.R.H., 589 S.W.3d 62 (Mo. App. E.D. 2019)*

**Cultural conversation:** The United States was a trailblazer for the world when it created the first federal agency whose sole responsibility was focusing on the needs of children. The Children's Bureau was created in 1912 to address the numerous concerns (child labor, orphan trains, etc.), but the first issue it tackled was the number of babies dying before the age of one.[7] Because of many efforts, childbirth rates improved for some—but not for all. Currently, black and Native women have the highest maternal and infant mortality rate in the nation.[8,9] This means black women and their babies are dying at a rate of over two times that of white women.

**Scriptures for further reading and reflection:**
- "So you have sorrow now, but I will see you again; then you will rejoice, and no one can rob you of that joy." **John 16:22**
- "Then Jesus said, 'Come to me, all of you who are weary and carry heavy burdens, and I will give you rest. Take my yoke upon you. Let me teach you, because I am humble and gentle at heart, and you will find rest for your souls. For my yoke is easy to bear, and the burden I give you is light.'" **Matthew 11:28–30**
- "He heals the brokenhearted and bandages their wounds." **Psalm 147:3**

---

7   *The Children's Bureau Legacy: Ensuring the Right to Childhood.* Administration for Children and Families, U.S. Department of Health and Human Services, 2013. https://www.childwelfare.gov/more-tools-resources/resources-from-childrens-bureau/cb-ebook/ Accessed 21 November 2020

8   Ely DM, Driscoll AK. Infant mortality in the United States, 2018: Data from the period linked birth/infant death file. National Vital Statistics Reports, vol 69 no 7. Hyattsville, MD: National Center for Health Statistics. 2020.

9   https://www.cdc.gov/media/releases/2019/p0905-racial-ethnic-disparities-pregnancy-deaths.html Accessed 22 November 2020

## What's your perspective?

# Perspective 4—Forbidden Children: Genesis 6:1–4

*Born a Crime* a 2016 autobiography

The earth was rocking and rolling. People were procreating and populating the earth. However, there was an issue: The "sons of God" saw the beautiful women on the earth and began taking them as wives and having intercourse with them. This resulted in children being born known as "giant Nephilites," who are described as the heroes and famous warriors of ancient times.

- Have you ever experienced feeling like you stuck out?
- How do our children feel when they notice they are different?
- As believers, should we blend in or stick out?

**Parenting perspective:** We have four children, and I recall when our oldest daughter noticed her skin tone. She was in kindergarten and made the curious statement, "Mama, I am the only one with chocolate skin color in my class." I asked her, "Well, what do you think about that?" She told me, "Well, it's OK. I think it's how God made me."

"That's right, darling, and He made you on purpose, and you're smart and beautiful," I explained. She went on, "But I look different…my skin is darker." I paused and said, "It's because you *are* different. No person is the same on the outside or inside, and you are no better and no worse than anyone else."

**BSP takeaway:** Be careful trying to blend in; it can send a message that different is bad. God made us all unique.

**A legal case:** A previous award was upheld for an African American woman who was awarded $1.3 million in actual damages and $7.2 million in punitive damages on her claims regarding racial discrimination and retaliation. Her employer subjected her to a toxic work environment for nearly twelve years, which included repeatedly using hate speech, denying her promotions she qualified for (and for which she was the top candidate once interviewed), forcing her to commute nearly two hours three days a week after she filed a complaint with HR, taking away her office, and repeatedly intimidating and using foul language when addressing her.

*McGaughy v. Laclede Gas Co., ED107498 (2020)*

**Cultural conversation:** As outlined in the above legal case, people experience racism and being treated unequally in many different settings. Fighting through unfair treatment can take a toll on the mind, body, and soul. Safe environments are needed to continue fighting for equity. How are we creating safe environments for this conversation in our local churches?

**Scriptures for further reading and reflection:**
- "We even saw giants there, the descendants of Anak. Next to them we felt like grasshoppers, and that's what they thought, too!" **Numbers 13:33**
- "The world would love you as one of its own if you belonged to it, but you are no longer part of the world. I chose you to come out of the world, so it hates you." **John 15:19**
- "Don't copy the behavior and customs of this world, but let God transform you into a new person by changing the way you think. Then you will learn to know God's will for you, which is good and pleasing and perfect." **Romans 12:2**

**What's your perspective?**

_____

_____

_____

_____

# Perspective 5—Set Apart: Genesis 6:9–22

*Evan Almighty* a 2007 movie

When God told Noah to build the ark, Noah could have refused. *Evan Almighty*, a modern-day movie, is an adaptation of the Great Flood story (Genesis 6–10). It gives a great present-day visual of the ridicule Noah and his family must have experienced while they spent years building the ark.

- How do you think Noah's family felt while they were building the ark?
- Have you ever made a decision other people did not understand? Why did you make the decision?
- How does your family do things differently than the rest of the world?

**Personal perspective:** My brothers and I had access to one television growing up, and we had no cable. At school, I felt that I didn't fit in, and I definitely didn't understand the references to music videos and songs. However, it forced me to cultivate a new hobby, which was a love for reading. I also developed friendships with people who had similar interests. We exchanged books and created our own little world.

**BSP takeaway:** Do what God has told you to do, and remember to make God's opinion of you the most important.

**A legal case:** Imagine if Noah would have needed a boat permit! In this legal case, Krahn was ticketed because he parked his truck and boat trailer in a parking lot without a boat permit. Krahn sued, saying his constitutional rights were violated because it was restricting his access to public waters. The court ultimately disagreed for a couple of reasons, one being that the city allowed free street parking next to the lot.

*Village of Winneconne v. Krahn, 751 N.W.2d 903 (Wis. App. 2008)*

**Cultural conversations:** The difficult part of obeying God and not people is that we will inevitably disappoint people we love and respect. Think of the student who believes God is telling her to pursue a career in the arts but is met with loving opposition from relatives who tell the student to choose a career that will generate income and help the family. Choosing to obey God is not always easy. Sometimes seeking approval from people can get in the way of seeking God's approval.

**Scriptures for further reading and reflection:**
- "But you belong to God, my dear children. You have already won a victory over those people, because the Spirit who lives in you is greater than the spirit who lives in the world. Those people belong to this world, so they speak from the world's viewpoint, and the world listens to them." **1 John 4:4–5**
- "Don't copy the behavior and customs of this world, but let God transform you into a new person by changing the way you think. Then you will learn to know God's will for you, which is good and pleasing and perfect." **Romans 12:2**
- "But you are not like that, for you are a chosen people. You are royal priests, a holy nation, God's very own possession. As a result, you can show others the goodness of God, for he called you out of the darkness into his wonderful light." **1 Peter 2:9**

**What's your perspective?**

# Perspective 6—The First Quarantined Family: Genesis 7–8

*I am Legend* a 2007 movie

Noah and his entire family were on the boat for over three hundred days. The entire earth was covered with water. Venturing outside of the ark would have meant certain death for Noah and his family. Not only was this family together at sea for over three hundred days, but there also were countless animals on the same boat. Noah and his family experienced the first quarantine.

- How do you think Noah and his family were able to maintain their sanity after being on a boat for three hundred days?
- What negative experiences do you believe they faced?
- What are positive experiences they likely encountered?

**Personal perspective:** COVID-19 ravaged the entire world beginning in December 2019. Schools closed, businesses were declaring bankruptcy, and many people have unfortunately lost their lives. Although the world feels chaotic at times, we find comfort in knowing there will be a rainbow (see Genesis 9:13) and that God will provide solace to all the grieving families who have experienced sickness and loss.

**BSP takeaway:** There is always something to be thankful for—always. Sometimes you have to look a little harder to find it.

**Legal case:** A mother was convicted in 1913 of violating the health officers' quarantine order. She and her children were thought to have scarlet fever and were ordered to quarantine to prevent the spread of the disease. Her children were found outside "mingling with others," and the mother was brought up on charges. The state failed to prove the mother allowed the children to go outside the home. The case was reversed. *State v. Rackowsk, 86 Conn. 677, 677, 86 A. 606*

**Cultural conversation:** Why do you think there is such a deep division about how to best combat COVID-19 in America? To restate two positions, some individuals believe Americans are entitled and operate in self-interest, which is why there has been such a controversy with stay-at-home orders and mask mandates. Others believe America is sliding into a dictatorship and our immediate liberty and freedom are at stake if we do not resist. What are your thoughts? What does the Bible say about this matter?

**Scriptures for further reading and reflection:**
- "Don't worry about anything; instead, pray about everything. Tell God what you need, and thank him for all he has done. Then you will experience God's peace, which exceeds anything we can understand. His peace will guard your hearts and minds as you live in Christ Jesus." **Philippians 4:6–7**
- "Always be joyful. Never stop praying. Be thankful in all circumstances, for this is God's will for you who belong to Christ Jesus." **1 Thessalonians 5:16–18**
- "Do not be afraid or discouraged, for the LORD will personally go ahead of you. He will be with you; he will neither fail you nor abandon you." **Deuteronomy 31:8**

**What's your perspective?**

# Perspective 7—Who Snitched? Genesis 9:18–24

*Goodfellas* a 1990 movie

Noah is the first documented vigneron, or winemaker, in the Bible. In Genesis 9, Noah is found cultivating the ground where he planted a vineyard. Then Noah begins consuming the product. Noah becomes so drunk, he strips and is found lying naked in his tent. Ham finds his father and runs to tell his brothers what he saw. Shem and Japheth cover their father's nakedness with a robe. When Noah wakes from his drunkenness, he "learns" what his youngest son, Ham, did. How do you think Noah finds out what happened?

- Were Ham's actions illegal?
- Were Ham's actions immoral?
- Should someone have told Noah what happened?

**Legal perspective:** There is a terrible saying that "snitches get stitches," which means if people begin divulging information to the authorities, there will be violent consequences for the one who "told it." This saying is a variant in many circles, but it is basically a code of silence—even when someone has done something illegal. This has caused many families to not have the justice they deserve because there was no cooperating witness.

**BSP takeaway:** Too often we retell a juicy story to a willing audience. Before repeating something that we have seen, we must ensure the following: (1) that we are telling the truth, (2) that it's necessary, and (3) that God has led us to repeat the information.

**Legal case:** You can't legally threaten to harm people in order to stop them from reporting a crime. Mr. Sabato, a criminal defendant, appealed a criminal conviction of

intimidating a witness. The defendant (Mr. Sabato) found out a person named Mason gave a statement to the police implicating Mr. Sabato of a crime. Mr. Sabato sent Mason the following Facebook messages: "I thought we were straight and u wouldn't be dumb enough to write a statement after telling u that day what we did to the last snitch... [U]r gonna get treated like a snitch...[U] best be ready for the [explicit language] u got urself into...I'd watch out if I were u..." Mr. Sabato's conviction of intimidating a witness was upheld on appeal.
*State v. Sabat, 321 Conn. 729, 749, 138 A.3d 895, 907*

**Cultural conversation:** There are articles[10] that point to a phenomenon of undocumented immigrants not reporting crime when they have been victimized. The Department of Homeland Security even has information about this concern on their website.[11] The articles believe it is because of the threat of deportation an undocumented family may face. Ultimately, families are choosing between pursuing justice for the alleged crime committed and potentially being deported.

**Scriptures for further reading and reflection:**
- "An honest witness tells the truth; a false witness tells lies." **Proverbs 12:17**
- "We are careful to be honorable before the Lord, but we also want everyone else to see that we are honorable." **2 Corinthians 8:21**
- "There are six things the LORD hates— no, seven things he detests: haughty eyes, a lying tongue, hands that kill the innocent, a heart that plots evil, feet that race to do wrong, a false witness who pours out lies, a person who sows discord in a family. My son, obey your father's commands, and don't neglect your mother's instruction." **Proverbs 6:16–20**

---

10   See https://www.nytimes.com/2018/06/03/us/immigrants-houston-domestic-violence.html, https://www.aclu.org/sites/default/files/field_document/rep18-icecourthouse-combined-rel01. pdf, and https://www.policechiefmagazine.org/encouraging-crime-reporting-by-immigrants/. Accessed November 22, 2020

11   https://www.dhs.gov/immigration-options-victims-crimes

## What's your perspective?

# Perspective 8—Intoxicated: Genesis 9:18–29

*Flight* a 2012 movie

Noah drinks so much wine that he is naked and unconscious. Noah likely wakes up with a hangover. Someone tells Noah what happened (Ham, not honoring Noah, his father, by telling his other two brothers), and in Genesis 9:25, Noah begins speaking things into Ham's life. Noah doesn't say, "Ham, you are cursed." Noah begins cursing his own grandchild, Canaan.

- What is a cursing?
- Should parents curse their children?
- Why do you think Noah cursed his grandchild for the parent's action?

**Legal and social perspective:** Driving while intoxicated is a crime. Many lives have been changed forever because of a decision to get behind the wheel while inebriated. Driving with any type of impairment can be illegal and dangerous. The words people speak while intoxicated can be just as deadly and abusive. Words do not leave external scars; instead, they leave internal ones.

**BSP takeaway:** Decisions made intoxicated will often be the wrong ones.

**Legal case:** A couple was married and divorced within a year and had a child. The father moved away with the child and began living with his longtime companion, "L. T." The father ingested a large amount of marijuana in 2013. He began having a drug-induced psychotic episode. He became violent with L. T. He ran into traffic and was arrested for assault, disorderly conduct, public intoxication, and spousal abuse. A child-in-need-of care case was ultimately filed, and the father appealed the decision for the court to become involved in his family. The judge ruled court involvement was necessary because of the abovementioned criminal acts and a history of suicide attempts, hallucinations, and lack of medical care by the father.

*In re G.J., B256004 (2015)*

**Cultural conversation:** Many justifications were falsely perpetuated to permit slavery. This justification has included using the Bible to defend the evil actions of enslaving another human being. Scholars, specifically those with a perverse incentive to build prosperity on the backs of enslaved people, used Genesis 9:20–27 to justify the enslavement of African people.[12] However, this argument is flawed in several ways: (1) It's typically known as the "curse of Ham," however, Noah did not curse Ham. He cursed Canaan, Noah's grandson.[13] (2) The name "Ham" was interpreted as meaning "black"—this was an incorrect interpretation. (3) Black then became synonymous for cursed—this is an inaccurate interpretation.[14] (4) The first three sons of Ham are the ancestors of Africa, yet Canaan did not settle in Africa.[15] (5) Finally, what God has blessed, no person can curse.[16]

**Scriptures for further reading and reflection:**
- "The tongue can bring death or life; those who love to talk will reap the consequences." **Proverbs 18:21**
- "What sorrow for those who are heroes at drinking wine and boast about all the alcohol they can hold. They take bribes to let the wicked go free, and they punish the innocent. Therefore, just as fire licks up stubble and dry grass shrivels in the flame, so their roots will rot and their flowers wither. For they have rejected the law of the LORD of Heaven's Armies; they have despised the word of the Holy One of Israel." **Isaiah 5:22–24**

---

12  For a comprehensive study: Goldenberg, David. "*The Curse of Ham: Race and Slavery in Early Judaism, Christianity, and Islam*" Princeton University Press (August 7, 2005).

13  See Genesis 9:25

14  Whitford, David. "A Calvinist Heritage to the 'Curse of Ham': Assessing the Accuracy of a Claim about Racial Subordination." *Church History and Religious Culture*, vol. 90, no. 1, 2010, pp. 25–45. JSTOR, www.jstor.org/stable/23923454. Accessed 20 Nov. 2020.

15  *See* The Africa Study Bible, NLT. Oasis International 2017, online pdf pp 83 African Touch Point: https://files.tyndale.com/thpdata/firstChapters/978-1-4964-2471-6.pdf Accessed 22 Nov. 2020.

16  "But how can I curse those whom God has not cursed? How can I condemn those whom the LORD has not condemned?" Numbers 23:8. See Genesis 9:1 and Galatians 3:27-29

- "But now is the time to get rid of anger, rage, malicious behavior, slander, and dirty language." **Colossians 3:8**

**What's your perspective?**

_____

_____

_____

_____

# Perspective 9—The Power of Communication: Genesis 11

*Set It Off* a 1996 movie

The Tower of Babel is an example of what happens when people come together with a common goal, clear communication, and focused energy. People all over the world migrated to the east and settled there together. However, their motives were questionable, and God confused the languages to end the project. After this occurred the people spread out over the earth.

- How were the people of Babylonia's motives questionable?
- How important are common goals, clear communication, and focused energy in families, churches, and businesses?
- Have you ever been confused about what someone was asking you to do? How did it make you feel?

**Social service perspective:** In every state there is a social service agency that evaluates child abuse and neglect allegations and adult abuse allegations, offers vocational rehabilitation services, and provides economic assistance. Economic assistance includes food, cash, utility assistance through federal moneys, and employment opportunities. Picture what happens when you walk into this agency and have no idea how to ask or receive help. Your family may need food, or perhaps you need employment assistance. The agency works to remove barriers to families receiving assistance. One of the barriers can be language. In one of my offices, there are dozens of languages spoken within the community. The agency contracts with language-service providers to offer interpretation services for families.

**BSP takeaway:** Without a shared understanding of what is needed, people are not able to receive the help they need and complete projects in a timely manner.

**Legal case:** On June 28, 2000, a man called 911 to report a disturbance. The 911 operator was unable to understand him because of a language barrier. Not knowing what to expect, three police officers went to the residence. Once they arrived, the officers knocked on the door and identified themselves. No answer. A neighbor came out and told the officers she saw two individuals flee thirty minutes prior. They heard commotion and entered the residence. Once they entered, the officers saw a man trying to escape. They also saw guns and drugs. All three people were charged, but two were still at large and were never brought to trial. Diane, the one convicted, argued on appeal the officers violated her Fourth Amendment right of unlawful searches and seizures and the police should have never entered the residence. The court ruled based upon exigent circumstances, the unclear 911 call for help, and the commotion that the officers had a duty to enter the premises, where they discovered the drugs and gun.
*State v. Portes, 840 A.2d 1131 (R.I. 2004)*

**Cultural conversation:** I have heard it said, "If you live in this country (America), you should speak the language (English)." What are your thoughts on this sentiment? Why? What do you think someone with the opposite opinion would say is their reasoning?

**Scriptures for further reading and reflection:**
- "How wonderful and pleasant it is when brothers live together in harmony!" **Psalm 133:1**
- "Two people are better off than one, for they can help each other succeed. If one person falls, the other can reach out and help. But someone who falls alone is in real trouble. Likewise, two people lying close together can keep each other warm. But how can one be warm alone? A person standing alone can be attacked and defeated, but two can stand back-to-back and conquer. Three are even better, for a triple-braided cord is not easily broken." **Ecclesiastes 4:9–12**
- "Fools have no interest in understanding; they only want to air their own opinions." **Proverbs 18:2**

## What's your perspective?

# Perspective 10—Childless: Genesis 11:30

*The Help* a 2011 movie

Sarai is the wife of Abram. In the next verse, we learn she is unable to become pregnant and has no children.

- Is childbearing an identifier for women?
- When people choose not to have children, does this bother you?
- Is there shame for couples who do not have children?

**Personal perspective:** I interviewed a family member who wanted to have a child but was unable for over seven years. "I felt ashamed, as if something was wrong with me, or as if I was unworthy. People would ask when I was going to have a baby, and it was embarrassing. I thought I was unworthy in the eyes of God and felt like I was not a whole woman," she explained. "When people would ask, I would make excuses like 'We are enjoying each other,' or just smile and not saying it's going to happen. But the hardest part was seeing other women with children or pregnant and knowing there was a possibility I would never experience that joy," she expressed. "What helped you?" I inquired. "Encouragement and support from family, not constant questions or looks as if something were wrong with me. Also, a young lady shared her testimony online of her struggle with infertility, and she spoke life into my situation by being honest and not hiding."

**BSP takeaway:** Starting a family is a personal decision. Unless you have an intimate relationship with a person, consider not asking couples and women when they intend on having children. We never know people's struggles, desires, or ultimate destiny.

**Legal case:** Gloria Williams made national news when it was discovered she stole a newborn baby from a Jacksonville, Florida, hospital. The crime was not discovered until the child was eighteen years old. Williams entered a plea with the guarantee her prison sentence would be no longer than twenty-two years. The judge sentenced her to eighteen years in prison. She appealed, arguing the sentence of eighteen years was cruel and unusual punishment, given she had taken excellent care of the child. When she took the child, she had just suffered a devastating miscarriage, and she was likely suffering from postpartum depression and not in her right mind. The appeals court denied her motion and ruled the sentence was lawful.

*Williams v. State, 44 Fla. L. Weekly D 1943, 276 So.3d 499 (Fla. App. 1 Dist. 2019)*

**Cultural conversation:** Two words have generated a lot of conversation within the faith community. Birth control. Some believe the decree given to Adam and Eve and Noah to "be fruitful and multiply" is an applicable commandment today. Others believe this commandment was given because the earth was unpopulated at this time and they needed to repopulate the earth. Has birth control been discussed in your family? Do you believe taking birth control is a sin or a personal choice?

**Scriptures for further reading and reflection:**
- "Whatever is good and perfect is a gift coming down to us from God our Father, who created all the lights in the heavens. He never changes or casts a shifting shadow." **James 1:17**
- "Thank you for making me so wonderfully complex! Your workmanship is marvelous—how well I know it." **Psalm 139:14**
- "God blesses you who are hungry now, for you will be satisfied. God blesses you who weep now, for in due time you will laugh." **Luke 6:21**

**What's your perspective?**

**Visit the website: www.biblestudyperspectives.com**
Join the Jury today- find out more details at
www.biblestudyperspectives.com


**Follow Shanelle on social media:**
**Facebook:** https://www.facebook.com/BSPJURY
**Instagram:** @ShanelleDupree
**Twitter:** @ShanelleDupree

Made in the USA
Monee, IL
16 May 2021

67679671R00025